من قصص
الأنبياء ...في القرآن

Yusuf
PBUH

I0457644

يُوسُفُ

عليه السلام

FROM PROPHETS
STORIES
IN THE QUR'AN

Prepared by:
Noha Elmouelhi
and Dr. Mohamed El Mouelhi

إعداد: نهى المويلحي ود. محمد المويلحي

To my wonderful daughters. -N.E.

To My Grandchildren, My Inspiration. -Giddo M.

Text Copyright © 2023 by Noha Elmouelhi and Mohamed El Mouelhi.
Artwork Copyright © 2023 by Hossam El Mouelhi and Donia Farouk.

All Rights Reserved. No part of this book may be reproduced, transmitted, or stored in an information retrieval system in any form or by any means, graphic, electronic, or mechanical, including photocopying, taping, and recording, without prior written permission from the publisher.

جميع الحقوق محفوظة.

يوسف
عَلَيْهِ السَّلَامُ

ISBN 978-1-959536-02-4
First edition 2023

Published by Honey Elm Books LLC
www.HoneyElmBooks.com

Yusuf PBUH

يوسف عليه السلام

Editing: Noha Elmouelhi

Artistic Preparation: Hossam El Mouelhi - Donia Farouk

تحرير: نهى المويلحي

الإعداد الفني: حسام المويلحي- دنيا فاروق

Allah tells us in the Quran

that Prophet Yusuf's story is the best of stories.

One of the amazing things about this story

is that it is one full story.

Most of the Quran presents short parts of stories,

where we only get a glimpse or a small scene from

someone's life.

Surat Yusuf, however, is the full story told in order

with many ups and downs in his life that we get

a chance to "visualize" as we see a movie.

يخبرنا الله سبحانه وتعالى فى القرآن عن قصة النبى يوسف وكونها من أحسن القصص، ومن الاشياء المدهشة أن هذه القصة وردت كاملة فى سورة يوسف بينما معظم قصص الأنبياء ورد منها أجزاء قصيرة فى مواضع مختلفة فى القرآن. ولكن سورة يوسف جاءت بقصة مرتبة وكاملة بما فيها من التقلبات والمحن التى مر بها فى حياته كأننا نعيش معه كل لحظة وكأننا نتابع فيلما سينيمائيًا .

Yusuf is the son of Yaqub,
peace be upon them (pbut).
Yusuf grew up in a large family
with 11 older brothers and had a special place
in his father's heart.

تربى يوسف بن يعقوب في أسرة كبيرة وكان له أحد عشر أخًا، وكانت له معزة خاصة عند والده.

One night,

Yusuf saw in a dream that the sun, the moon,

and eleven stars were all bowing to him.

He asked his father what it meant.

His father advised him to keep this dream a secret from

his brothers, so they wouldn't get jealous.

Yusuf's relationship with his brothers was a rocky

one throughout his life.

في إحدى الليالي رأى يوسف في منامه أن الشمس والقمر وأحد عشر كوكبًا
يسجدون له، وعندما إستيقظ من نومه سأل أباه عن معنى هذا الحلم، فنصحه
أبوه ألا يخبر إخوته بهذا الحلم منعًا لغيرتهم منه وحقدهم عليه. وقد كانت
علاقة يوسف بإخوته غير حميمة لسنوات عديدة.

"(Remember) when Yusuf said
to his father: `O my father! Verily,
I saw (in a dream) eleven stars and the sun
and the moon, I saw them prostrating to me.' "
(Yusuf: 4)

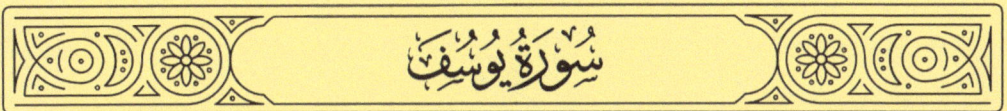

سُوۡرَةُ يُوۡسُف

بِسۡمِ ٱللَّهِ ٱلرَّحۡمَٰنِ ٱلرَّحِيمِ

إِذۡ قَالَ يُوسُفُ لِأَبِيهِ يَٰٓأَبَتِ إِنِّي رَأَيۡتُ أَحَدَ عَشَرَ كَوۡكَبٗا
وَٱلشَّمۡسَ وَٱلۡقَمَرَ رَأَيۡتُهُمۡ لِي سَٰجِدِينَ ٤

As time passed,
his brothers' jealousy increased.
They felt their father loved Yusuf more than them
and decided to get rid of Yusuf by throwing him
in a distant well to be found by a passer-by.
With Yusuf out of the way, they believed they would get
more attention and affection from their father.

مرت الأيام وإزدادت غيرة إخوة يوسف منه، فقد شعروا أن
والدهم –النبى يعقوب –يحبه أكثر منهم، فقرروا التخلص منه بإلقائه في بئر
بعيد ليعثر عليه أحد المارة ويأخذه بعيدًا عنهم، وبذلك يستحوذوا
على حب أبيهم ورعايته.

"One from among them said: `don't Kill Yusuf, but if you must do something, throw him down to the bottom of a well, he will be picked up by some caravan of travelers.' " (Yusuf:10)

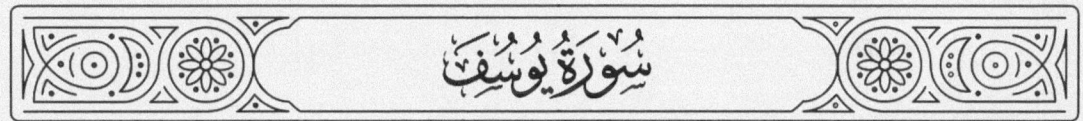

سُورَةُ يُوسُفَ

بِسْمِ اللَّهِ الرَّحْمَنِ الرَّحِيمِ

قَالَ قَآئِلٌ مِّنْهُمْ لَا تَقْتُلُوا۟ يُوسُفَ وَأَلْقُوهُ فِى غَيَبَتِ ٱلْجُبِّ يَلْتَقِطْهُ بَعْضُ ٱلسَّيَّارَةِ إِن كُنتُمْ فَٰعِلِينَ ۝

Yusuf's brothers
went ahead with their plan
and took Yusuf with them the next time
they went out to play.
They threw him into a well, and returned home crying and
claiming that Yusuf had been eaten by a wolf while he was
standing near their belongings.

قام إخوة يوسف بتنفيذ خطتهم للتخلص من يوسف، وأخذوه معهم ليلعب، ثم ألقوه
في بئر عميق، وعادوا الى البيت يبكون مُدعين أن الذئب أكل أخاهم يوسف
عندما تركوه عند متاعهم وهم يلعبون.

In order to fake their story,
they stained Yusuf's shirt with fake blood.
Their father was saddened by the loss
of his beloved son, but he did not believe them.

وجاءوا على قميصه بدم كذِب حتى يصدقهم أباهم يعقوب عليه السلام. وحزن أبوهم حزنًا شديدًا لفقدان إبنه الحبيب ولكنه لم يصدقهم.

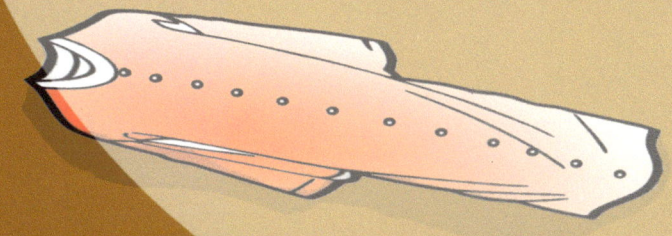

A caravan passed by
the well and found Yusuf.
They sold him to a rich man from Egypt,
known as 'Aziz of Egypt', and his wife.
They decided to take Yusuf in – perhaps he would be
of value to them in the future.

ومرت قافلة بالبئر وعثروا على يوسف، فأخذوه وباعوه
لرجل ثري من مصر –ويُعرف بإسم 'عزيز مصر'– وزوجته اللذين قررا شراءه
ربما ينفعهما في المستقبل.

All this time,
Allah was looking out for Yusuf
and helping him to grow into a strong young man
with wisdom far beyond his years and the ability
to interpret dreams – a skill that would be critical
to his future success.

وطوال هذا الوقت كان الله يرعى يوسف ويساعده على النمو ليصبح شابًا قويًا يتمتع بحكمة تفوق سنه، ومَنّ الله على يوسف بالقدرة على تفسير الأحلام وهي مهارة ستكون هامة لنجاحه في المستقبل.

Yusuf grew up
and became a very handsome man.
The lady of the house was not able to resist him,
and tried to tempt him.
Yusuf held fast to his faith, and asked Allah
to help him stay strong to overcome this temptation.

كبر يوسف وصار شابا وسيمًا جدًا، ومن شدة وسامته لم تستطع سيدة البيت
مقاومته وأخذت تحاول إغرائه بكل الطرق، ولكنه تمسك بإيمانه، وسأل الله
أن يعينه على البقاء قويًا للتغلب على هذه الفتنة.

She was insulted that Yusuf turned
her down and decided to accuse
him of tempting her.
She asked her husband to punish him.
Would Allah leave Yusuf alone to face this serious
accusation?

وشعرت سيدة البيت وقتها بالإهانة لعدم إستجابته لها، فقررت عقابه وإتهمته
بمحاولة الإعتداء عليها وطلبت من رب الأسرة التدخل وعقاب المخطئ، ولكن
هل سيترك الله يوسف البرئ وحده فى هذا الموقف الصعب؟

"So they raced with one another to the door, and she tore his shirt from the back. They both found her lord (i.e. her husband) at the door. She said: `What is the recompense (punishment) for who intended an evil act against your wife, except that he be put in prison or a painful torment?' " (Yusuf:25)

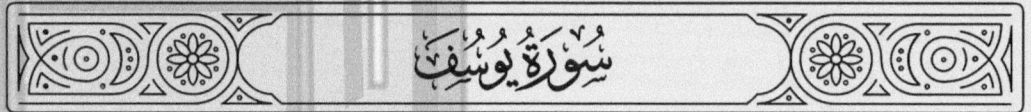

بِسْمِ اللَّهِ الرَّحْمَٰنِ الرَّحِيمِ

وَٱسْتَبَقَا ٱلْبَابَ وَقَدَّتْ قَمِيصَهُۥ مِن دُبُرٍ وَأَلْفَيَا سَيِّدَهَا لَدَا ٱلْبَابِ قَالَتْ مَا جَزَآءُ مَنْ أَرَادَ بِأَهْلِكَ سُوٓءًا إِلَّآ أَن يُسْجَنَ أَوْ عَذَابٌ أَلِيمٌ ۝

Of course not -

Allah does not like injustice!

So Allah revealed wisdom to a member

of the palace household.

He said they could determine who was guilty

by inspecting the location of the tear in Yusuf's shirt.

When they found the shirt was torn on the back, it confirmed

that she was the guilty one and that Yusuf was innocent

بالطبع لا، فإن الله لا يرضى الظلم! فأوحى الله إلى أحد أفراد القصر بالحكمة
لتحديد شخص المعتدى وذلك عن طريق معاينة مكان التمزق
فى قميص يوسف: فإن كان التمزق من الخلف فيوسف برئ
وهى المعتدية، وأما إن كان من الأمام فهو المعتدى وهى بريئة، وبهذا
ظهرت براءة يوسف إذ أن التمزق بقميصه كان من الخلف.

15

Word got out,
and the ladies of the town made fun
of her for being so easily attracted to a servant
in her household.
She tried to redeem herself and invited them over so they
would all see how handsome Yusuf was for themselves.
They all ended up cutting their fingers when they saw
how attractive he was.

وانتشرت الأخبار، وسخرت سيدات المدينة من ربة البيت لأنها كانت
سهلة الانجذاب إلى خادم في منزلها. فأرادت الإنتقام لنفسها
وإستعادة كرامتها، فقامت بدعوة هؤلاء السيدات إلى بيتها حتى يروا
مدى وسامة يوسف ليعذروها، وأنتهي بهن الأمر جميعًا بقطع أصابعهن
عند رؤية مظهره الجميل.

They threatened to imprison
Yusuf if he continued to resist them.
Yusuf made duaa to Allah to help him hold fast
to his faith, and that prison would be better
than being in the midst of such temptation all the time.
Even at such a young age, Yusuf was wise
and a strong believer, looking to Allah to help him.

وهددوا يوسف بالسجن إذا إستمر في مقاومتهن، وعندها دعا يوسف الله
أن يعينه ويقوى إيمانه، وأنه يفضل السجن على أن يكون في وسط
هذه الإغراءات طوال الوقت. لقد كان يوسف في هذه السن المبكرة حكيمًا
وقوي الإيمان طالبًا العون من الله.

Yusuf was sent to prison – even though
he had done nothing wrong.
He didn't dwell on his bad luck, but rather looked
for opportunities to help others.
He called on his prison mates to worship only Allah.

ودخل يوسف السجن مع أنه لم يخطئ، ومع هذا فإنه لم يتحدث
عن سوء حظه، بل كان يبحث عن فرص لمساعدة الآخرين، وكان يدعو
من معه فى السجن الى عبادة الله وحده.

Two men in prison with him approached him about dreams they had had.

One had dreamt that he was pressing grapes into wine, and the other had dreamt that he was carrying bread on top of his head and birds were eating from it.

وأثناء وجوده فى السجن كان معه رجلان سألاه عن تفسير أحلامهم إذ رأى أحدهم أنه يعصر عنبًا لعمل النبيذ، والآخر رأى أنه يحمل الخبز على رأسه وأن الطير تأكل منه.

Yusuf interpreted
their dreams for them – one would leave prison
and serve wine to a great leader;
the other would be crucified and birds would eat
from his head.
When it came time for the first prisoner to leave prison, Yusuf
asked him to remember him and to help him find a way out.

فسر يوسف معنى أحلامهما فقال: الأول يخرج من السجن ويقدم نبيذًا
لقائد عظيم، وأما الآخر فيُصلَب وتأكل الطيور من رأسه. وبعدها طلب
يوسف من زميله السجين الذي سيغادر السجن أن يتذكره ويساعده
في إيجاد مخرج له.

But Yusuf was destined to remain

in prison for a while longer.

Then, one day, the King dreamt of seven fat cows

being eaten by seven skinny ones, and seven fresh ears

of corn and seven others withered and dry.

No one was able to interpret the King's dream, but the King's

servant (the former prisoner) remembered how Yusuf had helped

him interpret his dream and told the King that Yusuf could help

them.

لكن كان مقدرًا ليوسف أن يبقى في السجن لفترة طويلة. ثم في أحد الأيام
رأى الملك في منامه سبع بقرات سمان تأكلها سبع بقرات هزيلة ، وسبع سنابل
خضراء من الذرة وسبع أخرى جافة، ولم يعرف أحد كيف يفسر
حلم الملك، وعندها تذكر خادمه كيف ساعده يوسف- وهما في
السجن- في تفسير حلمه من قبل، فأخبر الملك أن أحد المساجين
وإسمه يوسف يمكن أن يساعدهم
في تفسير حلم الملك.

21

They went to Yusuf in prison
to ask for his help.
Yusuf told them that they would have seven years
of prosperity followed by seven years of poverty
followed by a year of prosperity.

وبالفعل ذهبوا الى يوسف فى السجن وسألوه عن تفسير حلم الملك، فأخبرهم يوسف أنهم سيمرون بسبع سنوات من الرخاء تليها سبع سنوات من الفقر، ثم يأتى بعد ذلك عام من الرخاء.

This amazing gift from Allah saved Yusuf
from prison, cleared his name, and gave him one
of the most powerful positions - overseeing the vast
treasury of the kingdom.
All of this was a reward from Allah for his patience and faith.

وبفضل نعمة الله على يوسف – وهى القدرة على تفسير الأحلام– تم إنقاذ يوسف
من السجن وبرّاءته من تهمة الخيانة، ومنحه الملك أحد أقوى المناصب– وهى الأشراف
على خزينة المملكة. وهكذا حفظ الله سبحانه وتعالى يوسف وجازاه على
صبره وإيمانه بمكانة قوية عند الملك.

23

"And the king said:
`Bring him to me that I may attach
him to my person.'
Then, when he spoke to him, he said:
`Verily, this day, you are with us high in rank
and fully trusted.' (54) (Yusuf) said: `Set me over the
storehouses of the land; I will indeed guard them with full
knowledge' " (55) (Yusuf: 54-55)

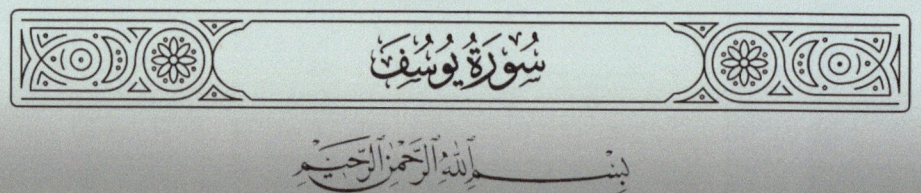

سُورَةُ يُوسُف

بِسْمِ اللهِ الرَّحْمَنِ الرَّحِيمِ

وَقَالَ ٱلْمَلِكُ ٱئْتُونِي بِهِ أَسْتَخْلِصْهُ لِنَفْسِي فَلَمَّا كَلَّمَهُ قَالَ
إِنَّكَ ٱلْيَوْمَ لَدَيْنَا مَكِينٌ أَمِينٌ ۝ قَالَ ٱجْعَلْنِي عَلَى خَزَآئِنِ ٱلْأَرْضِ
إِنِّي حَفِيظٌ عَلِيمٌ ۝

Several years later, Yusuf's brothers traveled
to Egypt to trade.

They didn't recognize Yusuf, but he recognized them.

Yusuf told them to bring their other brother next time or they
wouldn't receive a favorable trade for their goods next time.

وذات يوم قدم إخوة يوسف إلى مصر للتجارة، ولم يتعرفوا على يوسف
ولكنه عرفهم. وطلب منهم أن يحضروا أخاهم الآخر في المرة القادمة
ليسمح لهم بتلقي صفقات جديدة.

When the brothers returned home,
they told their father of their good fortune and how they
had been allowed to keep all of their goods in addition
to what they were gifted.

وعندما عاد الأخوة إلى بلدهم أخبروا والدهم –يعقوب عليه السلام– بحظهم السعيد
وكيف سُمِح لهم بالاحتفاظ بجميع ممتلكاتهم بالإضافة الى هداياه لهم.

They asked their father
to allow them to bring their youngest brother
on their next business trip.

Yaqub was so hesitant and sad to let another
beloved son leave him and to risk him being lost
like Yusuf was.

He reluctantly agreed.

وطلبوا من والدهم السماح لهم بأخذ الأخ الأصغر معهم عند ذهابهم
للتجارة بمصر. ولكن يعقوب – والد يوسف – كان مترددًا وحزينًا للغاية
للسماح لإبن محبوب آخر أن يتركه ويخاطر بفقده
مثلما حدث مع يوسف من قبل، وفى النهاية وافق
أبو يوسف على مضض.

The brothers returned to Egypt
and brought their goods to trade again.
As they were leaving after finishing their trade,
Yusuf arranged to have his youngest brother stay with him
under the guise of a theft.

عاد إخوة يوسف إلى مصر للتجارة مرة أخرى، وعند مغادرتهم بعد انهاء تعاملاتهم التجارية دبر يوسف حيلة لإبقاء أخيه الأصغر معه تحت ستار السرقة.

He ordered
his aides to hide the royal measuring
cup in his younger brother's belongings
to make it look as if he had stolen it.
The brothers were devastated to have
to leave their youngest brother and to risk
further saddening their father.

وحينها لم يستطع إخوته عمل أى شئ تجاه الحيلة المحكمة التى دبرها يوسف
إذ أمر مساعديه بإخفاء المكيال الملكى داخل متاع أخيه الأصغر ليبدو
كأنه سرقه، وشعر إخوة يوسف بالخيبة لأنهم اضطروا لترك أخاهم الأصغر
مما سيتسبب فى زيادة حزن أبيهم.

When the brothers returned
without their youngest brother, their father
was extremely sad and remembered his sorrow
over losing Yusuf as well – so much so that
he lost his vision.
The family encountered financial difficulties and the sons
needed to return again to Egypt to ask for help.

وحزن يعقوب عليه السلام حزنًا شديدًا وتذكر حزنه على فقدان يوسف
لدرجة أنه فقد بصره، وعانت الأسرة مشقة شديدة من القحط، وكان على الأبناء
العودة إلى مصر مرة أخرى لطلب المساعدة.

When the sons returned to Egypt
the third time, Yusuf revealed to them
who he really was.
They realized that Allah had chosen Yusuf because
of his faith and patience and that they were wrong.

وعاد الأبناء إلى مصر للمرة الثالثة، وعندها أظهر لهم يوسف حقيقته. فأدركوا أن الله سبحانه وتعالى قد اختار يوسف لإيمانه وصبره وأنهم كانوا على خطأ.

Yusuf told them to return back home
and to bring his father, mother,
and all the brothers back to Egypt to live.
Yusuf also sent with them his shirt to bring back
his father's vision – another divine miracle.

وطلب يوسف منهم العودة إلى ديارهم وإعادة والده ووالدته وجميع الإخوة
إلى مصر ليعيشوا معه، كما أرسل معهم قميصه لإلقائه على وجه أبيهم
ليستعيد بصره — وهذه معجزة إلهية أخرى نعمة من الله.

"Take my shirt, and cast it over the face of my father, he will become clear-sighted, and bring me all your family." (Yusuf:93)

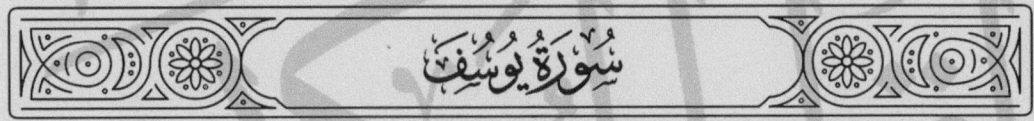

بِسْمِ اللّٰهِ الرَّحْمٰنِ الرَّحِيمِ

اذْهَبُواْ بِقَمِيصِى هٰذَا فَأَلْقُوهُ عَلَىٰ وَجْهِ أَبِى يَأْتِ بَصِيرًا وَأْتُونِى بِأَهْلِكُم أَجْمَعِينَ ۝

As Yusuf's family entered Egypt,
they bowed to him– thus bringing to life
the dream he had dreamt as a young boy of the sun,
the moon, and eleven planets bowing to him.

وعندما دخلت عائلته مصر، إنحنوا ليوسف، وبذلك تحقق حلم يوسف الذي
رآه وهو صبي صغير: رؤية الشمس والقمر وأحد عشر كوكبًا منحنين له.

It is only by the Grace
and Mercy of Allah that Prophet Yusuf was
able to be reunited with his youngest brother
and the rest of his family.
Yaqub was so patient and never lost faith in Allah;
such true faith was rewarded by being reunited with
both his lost sons, and clearing the jealousy among the
brothers.

وبفضل الله ورحمته سبحانه وتعالى تمكن يوسف من لم شمله مع أخيه الأصغر وبقية
أسرته. وقد كان يعقوب صبورًا ولم يفقد الإيمان بالله سبحانه وتعالى، وقد تمت
مكافأة هذا الإيمان الحقيقي بجمع شمله مع ولديه المفقودين وإزالة الغيرة
والحقد بين أبنائه.

35

PROPHET YUSUF PBUH WENT THROUGH MANY CHALLENGES WITH MANY LESSONS TO REMEMBER. HERE ARE A FEW OF THEM:

- Love between siblings is a powerful weapon to face hardships and adversities, no room for rivalry or jealousy.

- Strong faith and trust in Allah are important to help you get through difficult times.

- Don't dwell on your bad luck, but rather look for opportunities to help others and to use your talents.

- Everyone will be tested in life. How we react to these tests are what differentiates the believers from the non-believers.

مر سيدنا يوسف عليه السلام بصعاب كثيرة ذات دروس عدة مستفادة، وهذه بعض منها:

- المحبة بين الإخوة سلاح قوى لمواجهة المصاعب والشدائد ولا مكان للحقد أو المنافسة.
- الإيمان القوى والثقة بالله أساسيان للنجاة من المحن.
- لا تتحدث عن سوء حظك، بل إبحث عن فرص لمساعدة الآخرين واستخدام مواهبك.
- كل فرد سيختبر فى الحياة لبيان المؤمن من المنافق.

Lastly,
Yusuf's shirt played 3 important roles.

Do you know what these are?

The answer is on the next page…

وأخيرًا لعب قميص يوسف عليه السلام ثلاثة أدوار هامة.

أتعرف ما هى؟

الإجابة على الصفحة التالية…

The 3 important roles for Yusuf's shirt:

a) Fake evidence of Yusuf being eaten
by the wolf.

b) Proof of Yusuf's innocence when accused
by Al-Aziz's wife.

c) A way to cure his father's blindness.

الثلاثة أدوار التي لعبها قميص يوسف عليه السلام:

ا- دليل كاذب: يوسف أكله الذئب.

ب- دليل على براءة يوسف من إتهام زوجة العزيز
بالتعدى عليها.

ج- أداة لعلاج فقد بصر والده.

Yusuf PBUH,
one of the Prophets
in the Quran,
with examplary brotherly
relationship,
and a shirt of several roles

يوسف عليه السلام
هو أحد الأنبياء في القرآن
وذو العلاقة المثلى بين الإخوة
وصاحب القميص بمهام مختلفة

Watch a special reading of Yusuf PBUH by one of the authors!

Scan this QR code to access the video.

www.ingramcontent.com/pod-product-compliance
Lightning Source LLC
Chambersburg PA
CBHW041555120626
46551CB00002B/211